BATCHERY: VOLUME ONE

© 2018 Marcus V. Calvert

By Tales Unlimited, LLC.

Cover by Lincoln Adams

Edited by Alexandra Hupertz

INTRO

Here's how it works:

1.   Flip past the "Intro" section, to any random page. Pick a writing prompt that catches your eye. **These prompts aren't etched in stone**, so feel free to tweak them as you see fit. So, if you hate vampires, turn the vampire prompt into something else.

2.   From that prompt, create a short story with a beginning, middle, and end. **DO NOT** try to turn it into a novel (yet). Try to keep it under 3,000 words (unless the story goes there). The purpose here is to help you develop a stable writing routine, finish what you start, and discover your storytelling preferences.

3.   Try to complete the story in 5-7 days (or sooner, if you can). Go to another prompt and turn it into your next story. Then repeat this process 98+ more times.

4.   When you've written 100 or more stories, copyright them as one bulk property (Google the "**Library of Congress-Copyright Office**").

5.   Now do you write that novel? Nope. Pick 20-25 short stories and turn them into your first book. Try to find something they all have in common. My first anthology series ("Unheroic") was about unlikely heroes saving the day. Try to find a title that **ISN'T** on the Amazon website. Something unique, clever, and easy to pitch to an audience.

6.   Download some (free) Grammarly software. Use it on your work and find the typos. Google articles about "**fiction self-editing rules**" and "**grammar rules in fiction**." Surf the articles and compile a checklist. Will this replace your need for an editor? No. Still, you can erase some bad habits from your technique early on.

7.   Polish and re-polish your short stories until they're all as good as you can make them. Then polish them three more times. If you have to swap out a story or completely rework it, go ahead.

8.   Once done, you'll need two or three beta readers. I'd recommend hard-core movie geeks or anyone who can sniff out plot holes in anything they see. Offer payment and insist on a thorough read-through with sincere feedback. Do believe that good betas will find stuff that you missed.

9.   Start shopping around for editors—preferably someone who understands what you're trying to do. I'd recommend using a PayPal account (for easy payments and easier tracking, at tax time). To find that editor, start with word-of-mouth referrals from anyone you might know in the writing game. Also, you could plug "**fiction editor searches for beginners**" into Google. However you find that editor, ALWAYS pay by the word (not by the hour).

10.   Hit Google and type in "**free text to speech download**." Pick something that works well in Word and let it read your book to you. It's slow and plodding . . . but utterly worth the time. After the betas and editor are done with it, give your book one last listen—just in case some error slipped through the cracks.

11.   Where do you get your books published? That's up to you. If you're going through a traditional publisher, I'd start with Google and talk to writers who've gone through the process. From what I've seen, getting a publisher is a time-consuming nightmare. Personally, I'd rather self-publish (for now) because my books are mine and I can control how they're dropped. If a legit publisher tracks me down, then we'll talk.

Now, if you self-publish, do your homework.

As of this printing, I'd recommend Amazon KDP. Three reasons spring to mind.

One, readers like to buy their books/e-books from Amazon—for reliability, quality printing, and quick delivery. They only charge you (wholesale) for the books you buy, not for being on their website.

Two, publishers and self-publishers are dropping like flies in this competitive market. Amazon (for now) is the most stable way to self-publish.

Three, self-publishers have to charge more—both for their services and their books. They'll likely put your books on Amazon anyway, which only costs you more of your royalties. If you're worried about ownerships, copyright each of your books and buy ISBNs in bulk (Google **"Why should I buy ISBNs?"**).

12.   Whether you self-publish or not, consider banging out a few anthologies (with 20-25 short stories each). Folks still like to read short stories and will buy yours (if you hustle it right). Appealing cover art's a solid idea as well. Find an "eye candy" moment, in one of your stories, and make that your front cover. Sometimes, a great cover sells the book for you.

Why not start with that novel yet? Simple. The short stories are done and edited—just waiting to be sold. So sell 'em. I began with 180 short stories, self-published three anthologies, started an LLC., and hit every live-selling event I could find (from conventions to open mics to craft shows). I didn't bother with online marketing because the field's too crowded. Instead, I ordered a supply of books and signed up for vendor slots. Find the large crowds and/or go where the geeks gather. Both tend to be sympathetic to a passionate up-and-comer.

Find gigs, buy vendor spaces, and learn how to sell to people. If you want to wait until your second or third anthology is done, that's fine. You'll have more time to save up a war chest. My point is that an author with three books should sell better than an author with only one. Hustle your polished works with confidence and hone your chops. Then your fan base will gradually form and demand that novel.

13.   **NOW YOU WRITE THAT NOVEL.**
With all of those short stories you've knocked
down, a book concept should emerge. Also, you can
pluck choice ideas from past works (from plotlines
to odd characters to useful concepts).

If you can plot a book, good for you. Hit
Google for a plotting method that suits you.

If you can't outline to save your life—like
me—it'll be harder . . . but better. Why?
Because you have no idea how your book will
end. You'll knock around draft after draft until
the book's as good as you can make it. The
struggle is its own reward. Still, it wouldn't
hurt to look through Google, under "**Novel
Writing for Pantsers**." Maybe you'll find
something of use.

However you write your novel, expect to
write drafts you'll set aside. Save them anyway.
Flawed drafts might have choice bits that can
be salvaged later on. Label and save them in a
file somewhere (just in case). Then finish the
damn thing. Don't rush it. Rewrite whole
chapters (or even the whole thing) if you must.
When it's done, run it through the
polish/beta/edit process, copyright it, and slap a
cover on that puppy.

14.   Keep writing short stories (both to cook up new ideas and to stay sharp). Also, you'll need material for future anthologies, right? Imagine you're at a comic con table with two anthology series to your left and a novel series to your right. Toss in a "2 for $20" discount for flavor and make your pitch. True bookworms (or people shopping for them) will be sorely tempted to buy from you.

Many authors diss short stories. Ignore them because short stories sell very well in "live" settings. That's because anthologies have more possible pitches than a novel. Also, short stories are a faster proof of talent than a 70,000-word novel.

15.   If you decide to self-publish for the long-haul, write a will. Do estate planning and find an executor. If you don't have some kind of succession plan, your literary legacy might die with you—and that would be a shame.

16.   One Last **Purely Optional Step:** Pass this on to struggling writers. That friend or relative with more imagination than confidence. These prompts could help them.

Good Luck!

BATCH #1

01 – You're a mystical cop investigating a string of crimes committed with bars of alchemically created soap.

02 – A goofy Christmas tale about shopping for toys during a zombie apocalypse.

03 – A criminal mastermind's teenage kids throw an evil fundraiser to get their dad out of jail.

04 – You're interviewed by Anderson Cooper on the 20th anniversary of aliens appointing you President-for-Life of Earth.

05 – A banished fantasy hero is offered a chance to return home and regain lost honor by slaying an unkillable monster.

06 – You're a reporter doing a piece on a pair of popular super heroes undergoing a bitter divorce.

07 – A wrongfully-executed inmate haunts/kills jury members because of their sloppy deliberation.

08 – Imagine driving home in an America where road rage is perfectly legal (between the hours of 5 to 7 p.m.).

09 – You see a dog get popped by a hit-n-run driver and then die on the road . . . followed by eight tiny escape pod launches into the air.

10 – At high noon in an Old West ghost town, two rival super spies from [insert countries] square off (gadgets and all) to determine the world's best super spy.

BATCH #2

11 – An A-list actor's traumatic brain injury results in him thinking that he's his last movie character: the one he spent a year mastering with elite experts from around the world.

12 – An aging, decadent super hero hosts a reality show called, "Who Wants To Be A Sidekick?" In tonight's season finale, 3 remaining young supers compete to be his sidekick.

13 – The finest sword duelists in the world are summoned to a remote monastery for a series of one-on-one duels . . . where the winner gets to arrange the next century of world history.

14 – A Marine gunny is doing a presentation in his son's class when a deranged shooter breaks into the school.

15 – While hiking through the woods, two college frat boys stumble across an imminent mob execution and then . . .

16 – A down-and-out rapper gets offered wealth and fame by the Devil himself—for the usual price.

17 – A thief steals a billionaire's lucky statue (which comes to life and begs for help).

18 – A newbie fan stumbles onto an underground super villain Fight Club.

19 – An undead Serbian sniper stalks the NATO platoon that killed him.

20 – Jesus returns to Earth during the Great Depression.

BATCH #3

21 – You're a realtor trying to knowingly sell a haunted house to a loving couple and their two adorable kids.

22 – You're an Old West serial killer who's offering outlaws peace of mind by killing bounty hunters—as long as the price is right.

23 – You happily tag along with a bunch of hunters who kill the homeless . . . but the next target just happens to be your closest childhood friend.

24 – A group of mystics holds a friend's bachelor party in a pocket dimension.

25 – There's a fracking-related earthquake, which unleashes a dormant breed of oversized monsters upon your town.

26 – You're jogging along with your iPhone, listening to a warning about randomly-appearing temporal rifts . . . when you run through one.

27 – You're a judge at a beauty contest for mythical creatures.

28 – A year into a fall-of-civilization Apocalypse, you're a con artist who finally tracks down the massive gang that murdered your wife and daughter—and they don't recognize you.

29 – You're sent back in time to protect Christopher Columbus from Native American temporal terrorists who intend to kill him in the cradle.

30 – While biking across Colorado, you get on the good side of a bunch of spectral bikers who decide to "initiate" you into the gang.

BATCH #4

31 – A temporal physicist from the future figures out how to connect his/her computer into today's Internet, so that he/she can . . .

32 – A meteor lands near a small town and irradiates everyone in it—giving them super powers.

33 – A judge/former sniper moonlights as a vigilante, killing defendants he knows are guilty.

34 – A demon with a gambling problem bets his immortality for a prize too juicy to resist.

35 – Archaeologists find a crashed alien warship under the ruins of an ancient Mayan city.

36 – You and a group of hackers influenced the 2016 election. A year later, your hacker buddies start dying, one-by-one. Is someone coming for you?

37 – A serial killer (on his way to prison) gets abducted by the vengeful relatives of his many victims.

38 – A hitman impersonates the dentist of his next target—a cartel boss who's accompanied by guards at all times.

39 – A third-generation brat pack of grade school super villains strikes out on their own.

40 – A violinist can read the minds of anyone who hears her play, making her an ideal thief/spy.

BATCH #5

41 – What if there was a dating app to connect lonely singles with ghosts?

42 – A mad genius infects herself with a psychic plague which makes everyone's minds just as brilliantly twisted as her own.

43 – A health inspector notices that a hip new restaurant's serving up food laced with some kind of addictive agent.

44 – A foreign reporter unknowingly gets tagged by the CIA, who then arranges for his abduction by a group of terrorists (so they can shut them down).

45 – You start getting convincing Facebook messages from someone who's been dead for over a year.

46 – Someone accidentally gives you a 1-year free membership to a fitness club for super spies.

47 – You wake up in the middle of the night to the sound of your pets plotting for/against you.

48 – A horribly bullied girl graduates from high school in disgrace . . . only to return on the 20th anniversary with armed mercs at her back.

49 – You're on a quest to re-assemble a mystical artifact through which anyone could control the world.

50 – You've been clued into a reality show for assassins where the losing contestants wind up dead.

BATCH #6

51 – Imagine hunting a pack of werewolves through a post-Apocalyptic wasteland with no silver at hand.

52 – Inmates run a 20k through an abandoned, booby-trapped, company ghost town: with the winner getting his/her freedom.

53 – A billionaire goes out slumming and falls in love with a hooker having a bad day. He decides to help without flaunting his cash.

54 – Anyone this serial slasher kills comes back from the dead with his skills and worldview.

55 – A team of astronauts has to enter a booby-trapped (fake) asteroid, figure out who launched it, and then disarm it before it explodes in Earth's orbit.

56 – A bloodthirsty super villain has trouble maintaining his secret identity (of a loving family man/community activist).

57 – A young cattle baron with a lot of minions/connections/reach finds himself targeted by a vengeful U.S. Marshal—who happens to be his father.

58 – A group of aliens meet up to discuss the present and future of the human race . . . which they so easily control through social media.

59 – Thieves steal cursed money from a demon's bank: money that was meant to be dispersed among the masses.

60 – An AI-controlled android army appears from the future to attack the present Earth and take it over— but why?

BATCH #7

61 – You lost your memory and can't figure out who you were . . . until an old enemy comes along accusing you of being a demon.

62 – You're on a cruise liner that strays into hostile waters and gets attacked by their navy and air force.

63 – What if Roswell wasn't about UFOs but a crashed time-ship?

64 – Imagine you're in charge of a community college's curriculum for next year, tasked with introducing a major for Recreational Voodoo.

65 – A team of amateur kidnappers goes after a rich couple. They bungle it, the husband dies, and the wife escapes . . . then puts a contract on them.

66 – You're the spectral roadie for a five-person band of mystical musicians.

67 – Your kids go off to summer camp and come back different.

68 – You're taken to your bachelor party, get utterly wasted, and wake up in a fantasy world.

69 – You're so dangerous that your future (reformed) self-travels back in time to kill you.

70 – Your barbarian tribe's been decimated by a pack of vampires. Only you, a few badasses, and a powerful shaman remain. What happens next?

BATCH #8

71 – A school of dark magic actually kidnaps potential students . . . including your son.

72 – A dead super hero's butler publishes an exposé of his days running the lair.

73 – Stranded off-world behind enemy lines, a batch of space troopers stumble across a lightly-defended target: one worth risking certain death to go after.

74 – A limited-access suburb is created wherein every man/woman/child is hypno-trained with elite-level combat skills. Imagine one of them walking in on a crime!

75 – A demented mad genius threatens to drop a "Slut Bomb" over a major city unless his/her demands are met. What happens next?

76 – A scarred/disabled cop decides to get into the rap game. Out of spite, he proves himself to be better than any rapper ever.

77 – You're part of a team of super villains tasked with guarding a freighter's cargo, which wakes up mid-voyage.

78 – An underground reality show for super assassins.

79 – You don't know this but any story you write becomes reality. What sucks is that you like writing monster fiction.

80 – While clearing away a dead hoarder's home, your cleanup crew finds a priceless artifact.

BATCH #9

81 – The most powerful superhuman on Earth has a split personality, which swaps itself out on his birthday. In odd years, he's good. For even years, he's utterly evil.

82 – Tired of this conspiracy crap about Bigfoot, a geneticist creates his own breed and unleashes them upon rural America.

83 – You and your scumbag friends watch a super hero/villain throw down that flattens a few city blocks. As the dust settles and both sides leave, you decide to do some looting. Along the way, you come across . . .

84 – You and your crew are in the middle of the biggest score of your lives. Screw it up and your client's going to kill you all. Halfway through the smooth-running heist, your kid calls and tells you that she's just been kidnapped.

85 – You're walking home and stumble across a pregnant woman in labor. Her child's not human. Your intervention might determine the fate of galaxies.

86 – You're an E.R. physician in the middle of an emergency surgery when your patient starts beeping. That's right—the poor bastard's appendix is now covered by flashing lights, much like an armed explosive . . .

87 – Your dead grandma leaves you a muscle car. When you roll it into E-check, two guys try to kill you for the car, which guns them both down.

88 – You solve other people's problems (via persuasion, threats, or even murder). Business is good until one of your former clients outs you.

89 – You're a local news reporter getting the lowdown on a bank robbery thwarted by a circus clown, a drunken security guard, and an 8-year-old?!

90 – God's been on a creating spree, setting up several different Creations since He finished this one. Now he's back. Having looked around, the Almighty's reaction is . . .

BATCH #10

91 – A fantasy army's laying siege to a castle when this UFO crash lands in the castle courtyard.

92 – You and your pals do a home invasion on a Native American casino owner. Things get bloody. Next thing you know, you're being picked off by a bounty hunter (with shamanic roots) who tracks sins like a bloodhound.

93 – A convict on death row gets his last rites from a Wiccan, whose life he once saved. She "blesses" him so that after his execution, he wakes up in his pre-felon body with a clean slate and a second chance.

94 – You're walking home from Jujutsu class when you spot a bunch of thugs kills your dad (mugging). The world goes red and stays that way for a while. When you come to, you're across town. What's left of a SWAT team's wrestling you to the ground with bodies everywhere. What happened?

95 – The two guys seated in front of you are having a fight to the death . . . on a moving roller coaster.

96 – Corporate spies are after your prototype phone, which has an awesome crime-fighting app.

97 – You're waiting at a subway station when you notice a crowd forming. Apparently, a sobbing old mime is painting a breathtaking portrait of a young girl. What attracts the crowd is that he's not painting on a canvas. He's painting on *thin air* . . . without a brush.

98 – You creep into a gas station and fill your gas can. Halfway done, a panhandler comes up and pressures you into sparing him a few bucks . . . even though the world's 8 weeks into a zombie apocalypse.

99 – A trio of thugs break into a pet shop only to learn that the place is really a prison for mythical creatures.

100 – A domestic terror cell's operating under a farmhouse in South Dakota. You lead a raid on the site, only to discover that the terrorists are really...

BATCH #11

101 – A seemingly inept/clumsy villain kills your super hero partner, beats your ass, and gets away without a scratch. As you heal up, you pull together a profile of your enemy. What do you find?

102 – A drone pilot gets into an aerial dogfight with a live pilot, with the fate of thousands (perhaps more) at stake.

103 – The U.N.'s hired a pack of powerful mystics (from different disciplines) to help make this crazy-assed world more peaceful . . . by any means necessary.

104 – Over the last 10 years, you've been playing your favorite video game. Something about it's just timeless. While playing the game, someone walks in and kills you in cold-blood. The game pauses and your beloved game's protagonist steps out of your big screen television, keen on avenging you.

105 – An alien race challenges humanity to a *Battle of the Bands*. If they win, the human race becomes food stock—except for musicians, who will be kept as revered pets and bred for their awesome talent. If we win, they'll leave and never return.

106 – In a truly distant future, one half-crazed Swiss film director does a version of a 1950's doo-wop love story—with a horribly inaccurate string of historical records . . . which explains the Confederate ninja.

107 – You run a gang of freelance spies. Each is named after a card from the Tarot deck, with unique skill sets. They do your bidding. Have fun creating them...

108 – A day in the life of a used spy car dealer.

109 – You're a Secret Service agent who discovers that the President-Elect's a reactivated Chinese mole.

110 – A truly evil family opens a haunted hotel for normal guests . . . and entities looking for victims.

BATCH #12

111 – Your ex-husband just escaped from prison—after you discovered his mob ties and ratted him out to the FBI.

112 – It's May Day time in [insert college town]. The cops will be busy dealing with riotous students, who typically get stupid-drunk the week before finals. During the chaos, a clever bunch of thieves decides to pull off a daring heist.

113 – You've just retired from the military and brought your bomb-sniffing dog home with you. Happily taking a walk, you witness a violent crime and get involved. From then on, it's a soldier and her dog against [insert evil crew of bad guys].

114 – You track down a crazy old recluse whose moonshine you once sipped at a party . . . and beg for more. It allowed you to [insert ability].

115 – In the future, wealthy dying people can buy the right to have their memories inserted into death row inmates. A wealthy lawyer hops into the body of a street hitter and finds himself marked by old friends (and enemies) of his host.

116 – A pill promising super powers is introduced into the mainstream market. Side effects include . . .

117 – You're a foreign spy who steals an American prototype super fighter with fail safes already bypassed. Stealing it's only half the mission. Using it on a populated target's the next step.

118 – A super villain devises a sleep generator capable of knocking out an entire city with teams of bad guys ready to reap the easy pickings.

119 – You're bracing for an elimination tournament against the world's finest VR gladiators. The winner gets forty million Euros. The losers get sent home in body bags.

120 – A lonely lady art restorer finishes a portrait of an unknown gentleman, who politely thanks her when she's done.

BATCH #13

121 – A crime fighter learns a tattoo artist is using an ink laced with a zombie virus. All of her customers will die and become infected within the next 18 hours, unless . . .

122 – You're a cop who can see the past of anyone you touch (up to 24 hours).

123 – Time travelers go into the past to rescue Amelia Earhart.

124 – A day in the life, under Atlantian occupation, circa 1960's.

125 – Aliens decimate the human race, steal what they want, and leave the survivors in a true wasteland.

126 – Four smuggling outfits vie for a lucrative contract via a mad, cross-country race. Four cars, four drivers, and four pieces of contraband. The winning driver gets the contract.

127 – You're a slumlord peddling a foreclosed house that you're remodeling. A tenant wants to rent the place before it's finished at a lower price (for fixing it up). You agree, not knowing that the new tenants are [insert something messed-up].

128 – You're in a bar watching two experts have an intense televised debate about the Vampire Rights Amendment.

129 – You didn't know that your kid brother was a super spy until you borrowed his razor and almost blew out the bathroom wall.

130 – Someone left their jacket in a movie theater. You rifle the pockets and come away with a photo of a young woman with a knife at her throat and a time/place scribbled on the back. The meetup spot's across the street and the "when" is three minutes from now. Feeling brave?

BATCH #14

131 – You've been suckered into an underground RPG involving dice and multiple players. Anyone who completes the quest with a surviving character gets $1 million. The loser(s) get a bullet to the back of the head.

132 – In the future, a protestor's arrested for not carrying a concealed smartgun. Guns are so common that they even double as smartphones and serve as a form of ID.

133 – The world wakes up to learn that every American citizen on Earth is gone. The country and its territories are mostly vacant, with its vast resources utterly up for grabs.

134 – You lead a quest into a dragon's lair and find the dragon dead with eight eggs a-hatching . . . and a hoard large enough to kill for.

135 – Vampires the world over suddenly lose their infectious bite. Word gets out and the hunt begins because their value on the black market explodes overnight.

136 – During a zombie apocalypse, a "Snake Oil Salesman" rolls up to your walled encampment with everything one needs to survive in these dark times: from gun parts to door wedges to live skunks (which even zombies can't stand).

137 – A crashed alien colony ship is found in Vietnam, just after the Tet Offensive. Inside are carnivorous aliens (in stasis) who are awakened and begin to slaughter everyone they find, laying eggs in the bodies.

138 – The ghosts of two rival boxers possess two of their descendants to avenge the murder of a mutual friend.

139 – Space pirates fall through a wormhole and end up in the past . . . during the time of wood-and-scurvy pirates.

140 – The police arrest a mad bomber who sold rigged Christmas lights to over 100 families throughout the city. Each set's lined with explosives, which will go off when plugged in.

BATCH #15

141 – In the near-future, Presidential candidates are drafted, based on a smart program deemed to be "unhackable."

142 – Android factions have wiped out humanity and are now fighting among themselves for dominance of Earth and its stellar colonies.

143 – In the middle of a fantasy play, a wizard (in the audience) sends the cast to his fantasy homeworld— just to be a prick.

144 – A psi-virus is slowly turning every psychic on the planet into a raving killer. Worse, affected victims' powers are amped two-fold. You have to save the day.

145 – A cruel and mysterious foe forces a homeless vet to solve a string of riddles, each leading to a victim about to die.

146 – An occultist creates fake IDs that are TOO good. If he creates a fake driver's license for a 4-star general and gives it to a homeless child, the kid becomes the general for as long as the ID's in the kid's possession. Memories, skills, and fingerprints all copy over.

147 – A senior mobster facing jail time calls upon his godson (a grifter) to get him out of it.

148 – A jeweler offers dying clients a chance to cheat their afterlives by bonding their souls into jewels. What she neglects to mention is that these souls can now be tapped by those who know how . . .

149 – A vacationer runs afoul of a small-town meth gang—one where each member's a werewolf.

150 – You're part of the kidnapped audience for the pilot episode of an advice show, sponsored by a self-help guru-turned-psycho. It comes complete with armed thugs and a pair of kidnapped sidekicks who are about to be "advised" to death on national television.

BATCH #16

151 – A hitman and his estranged son decide to go out and bond . . . by wiping out a street gang.

152 – NASA sends a team of space marines to stop an inbound alien vessel, which is creating unnatural disasters all over the world.

153 – Something's in the attic, which ate the squirrels, raccoons, and the Orkin exterminator.

154 – There's a new space race to Mars after archaeologists find proof that mankind's a manufactured race. Apparently, there's a device designed to rule us— and it's on the Red Planet.

155 – A retired super henchwoman's working the honest life as a security guard until . . .

156 – A serial killer's targeting married men and taking their wedding bands as trophies.

157 – Every time you fall asleep, you end up in a twisted dream-based soap opera that seems to carry on without you during your waking hours. Among the cast is the true "love" of your life.

158 – The new kid on the block realizes that the local kids draw occult powers from . . .

159 – What if your daughter's prom date turned out to be a shapeshifting demon with [insert whatever] intentions?

160 – Souls of the heavenly dead are sent to Earth to endure the challenges necessary to attain angelhood.

BATCH #17

161 – You're a relatively happy pimp until a vampire comes along with the intention of "recruiting" your employees, bite-by-bite.

162 – You get mugged while walking your android defense dog.

163 – Some poor bastard runs his car into your police cruiser and begs you to shoot him . . . as he begins to transform.

164 – A new virus is going around the world. Those infected are beginning to grow, with the largest "patient" at 70 feet high.

165 – The President of the United States has you removed from Leavenworth. You're offered a full pardon for past crimes if you complete 10 messy kills for God and Country.

166 – Your car breaks down near a cult's walled compound/school of the mystic arts.

167 – It turns out that a comic book designer's main title is based on his very violent, super-powered past.

168 – You're a retired SEAL whose only child (a reporter) is mysteriously executed by . . .

169 – This human bounty hunter tries to bring in a captured super villain with everyone on their tails.

170 – You're a tourist in a long-closed prison. While on tour, the ghost of a dead inmate decides you're worth haunting.

BATCH #18

171 – What if your service animal was a hellhound?

172 – A pizza boy (delivery in hand) walks in on a murder.

173 – A crew of gas-masked terrorists storm a section of an airport and fill the place with an experimental mind control gas.

174 – Students are caught cheating by the most unforgiving of teachers. Wonder what the class was?

175 – Snowmen start climbing out of the snows around your rustic little village with the clear intention of killing everyone.

176 – The local mob boss forces himself on your kid sister, who ends up slicing him open. Now you're all that stands between her and violent payback.

177 – Two years ago, you drank a tiny bottle of unmarked booze and you've been drunk ever since.

178 – Scientists decipher the human DNA chain and discover something quite amazing: everyone's DNA determines their every action (from birth to death). In essence, reading one's DNA is the same as reading that person's exact fate.

179 – An ancient, giant alien battle robot rises from the sands of Egypt and decides whether or not to complete its programming.

180 – A lunatic genius created a device that can absorb 100% of a tornado's fury like a sponge. Rather than collect a Nobel Prize, he's "bottled" up X number of tornados, rigged them to explode, and has ransom demands in mind.

BATCH #19

181 – You almost get away with murder, only to face a mother-daughter team. The mom's a retired bounty hunter and the daughter's a detective prodigy.

182 – There's a wild game of keep-away, involving a home-made plaid shirt with top-secret code woven into its fabric.

183 – Imagine a case of sexually-transmitted vampirism.

184 – A DEA team raids a remote drug spot, only to get hit (and cut off) by a larger team tasked with taking them out.

185 – Imagine watching the once-in-a-decade race between weird scientists, mystics, and aliens.

186 – A hitwoman chases her former high school sweetheart across the Midwest.

187 – Alien terrorists slipped onto your space station with the intention of killing everyone on board.

188 – During D-Day, your squad's plane draws fire and the survivors bail out too soon . . . behind enemy lines.

189 – A wealthy televangelist moonlights as a vigilante.

190 – A baby genius builds a holographic army and invades the world.

BATCH #20

191 – A day in the life of an orderly in a super hero asylum.

192 – A firm supplies spectral bodyguards for well-paying clientele.

193 – A cop and a mob soldier put aside their differences to avenge the murder of an old friend from their childhood.

194 – A babysitting service for super hero/villain offspring.

195 – What if your decent singing voice drives people into a feral rage?

196 – You're at the mercy of your worst enemy who can't kill you because . . .

197 – The world's top 8 martial arts actors are kidnapped and forced to fight to the death in an underground tournament.

198 – You're fleeing a delivery room because the baby slid out, grew to the size of a male lion, and started eating your colleagues.

199 – How would Santa pull off Christmas after a zombie apocalypse?

200 – A pair of mortal enemies chase a single parachute out of a plane (at 17,000 feet), just before the plane explodes.

ABOUT THE AUTHOR

Marcus V. Calvert is a native of Detroit who grew up with an addiction to sci-fi that just wouldn't go away. His goal is to tell unique, twisted stories that people will be reading long after he's gone.

His books are available on Amazon.com and Kindle. You can also follow him on:

*Website: talesunlimited.net

*Twitter: https://twitter.com/MarcusVCalvert

*Facebook: Tales Unlimited – Author Page

*TikTok: talesunlimited

*YouTube: "Batchery Daily Prompt Disturbing Thought of the Day"

CURRENT TITLES

Short Story Anthologies

The Unheroic Series

Unheroic, Book 1
Unheroic, Book 2

The Book Of Schemes Series

The Book Of Schemes, Book 1
The Book Of Schemes, Book 2
The Book Of Schemes, Book 3

Novels

The I, Villain Series

I, Villain
Murder Sauce
Frag Code
Coin Game

Writing Guides

The Batchery Series

Batchery, Volume I
Batchery, Volume II

Made in the USA
Monee, IL
25 May 2022

96935416R00030